CLASSICAL COMPOSERS

Franz SCHUBERT

by Joanne Mattern
with Consultation by John Viscardi,
Executive Director of Classic Lyric Arts
illustrated by Marilena Perilli

Egremont, Massachusetts

Classical Composers has been produced and published by Red Chair Press Books for Young Readers:
Red Chair Press LLC PO Box 333 South Egremont, MA 01258
www.redchairpress.com

 Download a Free Activity Guide on our website.

For more information about Classic Lyric Arts, visit www.classiclyricarts.org.

Names: Mattern, Joanne, 1963- author. | Viscardi, John, consultant. | Perilli, Marilena, illustrator.

Title: Franz Schubert / by Joanne Mattern, with consultation by John Viscardi, executive director of Classic Lyric Arts ; illustrated by Marilena Perilli.

Description: Egremont, Massachusetts : Red Chair Press, [2026] | Series: Mattern, Joanne, 1963- Classical composers. | Interest age level: 008-012. | Includes bibliographical references and index. | Summary: Franz Schubert (1797–1828), an Austrian composer of the late Classical and early Romantic eras. Despite his short life of only 31 years, Schubert created more than 600 works, including operas, symphonies, sacred music and many pieces for chamber music.--Publisher.

Identifiers: LCCN: 2025939519 | ISBN: 9781967893126 (library hardcover) | 9781967893133 (paperback) | 9781967893157 (S&L ePub 3) | 9781967893140 (S&L ebook PDF) | 9781967893171 (audiobook)

Subjects: LCSH: Schubert, Franz, 1797-1828--Juvenile literature. | Composers--Austria--Biography--Juvenile literature. | CYAC: Schubert, Franz, 1797-1828. | Composers--Austria--Biography. | LCGFT: Biographies. | BISAC: JUVENILE NONFICTION / Music / Classical. | JUVENILE NONFICTION / Biography & Autobiography / Music. | JUVENILE NONFICTION / Biography & Autobiography / Performing Arts.

Classification: LCC: ML410.S3 M38 2026 | DDC: 780.92--dc23

Image credits: 4 Wilhelm August Rieder (1796-1880)/Courtesy of the Wien Museum; 6 Lisa Rastl/Courtesy of the Wien Museum; 14 The Picture Art Collection/Alamy; 20 Luisa Ricciarini/Bridgeman Images; 22 Chronicle/Alamy; 24 Look and Lear /Elgar Collection/Bridgeman Images; 26 Imago/Alamy; 30 Roy Harris/Shutterstock

Illustrations: Marilena Perilli, except p. 7 by Joe LeMonnier

Printed in the United States of America

0426 1P F26CG

Table of Contents

Nothing But Music 4

Back to School 14

Schubert's Concerts. 20

Beautiful Music 22

Beethoven's Biggest Fan 24

Schubert's Last Years. 26

Timeline 31

Glossary 32

Read More 32

Index 32

Nothing But Music

Franz Schubert wanted nothing more than to write and play music. This famous **composer** started playing music when he was very young. But few people thought he would ever become famous. Franz did not care. He only wanted to compose.

Franz Peter Schubert was born on January 31, 1797. He was born in a small town near Vienna, Austria called Himmelpfortgrund. Franz's parents had fourteen children. But only Franz, three older brothers, and one younger sister lived past childbirth.

Schubert's birthplace near Vienna.

B#

B SHARP: Franz's brother, Ignaz, started teaching him piano when Franz was just five years old.

N
NORWAY
SWEDEN
DENMARK
RUSSIAN EMPIRE
NETHER-LANDS
Hamburg
HANOVER
Berlin
UK
London
PRUSSIA
Warsaw
SAXONY
Paris
BAVARIA
Himmelpfortgrund
Vienna
FRANCE
SWITZ
AUSTRIAN EMPIRE
OTTOMAN EMPIRE
Rome
SPAIN
PAPAL STATES
TWO SICILIES

Franz's family loved music. They played music all the time in their home. Franz's father played the **cello**. He taught two of his sons to play violin. He taught Franz to play the **viola**. The four of them often played together in a **string quartet**.

B#

B SHARP: Franz wrote his first compositions for his family to play.

Franz also studied with the organist at the church in town. He learned to play the organ and the piano. He then learned to sing. Franz was very good with all music!

Franz had a beautiful singing voice. In 1808, he was chosen to go to a school called the Imperial and Royal Seminary. Franz soon sang in the **choir** at the school's church.

B#

B SHARP: One of Franz's teachers was Antonio Salieri. Salieri was a friend and **rival** to Wolfgang Amadeus Mozart.

Franz also played the violin at the Seminary. He joined the school **orchestra**. Franz played so well, the **conductor** made him the leader of the violins. Sometimes Franz conducted the orchestra when the conductor was away.

Back to School

Schubert loved school. All Schubert wanted to do was write and play music. Then something happened. His voice changed. It became deeper, which meant his time singing with the childrens' choir was finished. In 1813, he left school.

Schubert wanted to be a composer. But his father said no. He told Schubert that he could not make enough money as a musician. Schubert's father had another idea for his son.

Schubert's father ran a school. He hired Schubert to teach the little boys who went there. Schubert worked at the school until 1818.

Schubert spent his days teaching. The rest of the time, he composed music. But Schubert was very shy. He only played and sang his music for close friends.

B#

B SHARP: Schubert was considered to be short for a young man. His friends called him "Schwammerl." That means "Little Mushroom" in German.

Schubert wrote hundreds of music pieces called "lieder." "Lieder" (leader) is the German word for songs. Schubert liked to take poems and set them to music. He wrote more than 500 lieder.

Schubert's lieder were ground-breaking in vocal music. His most important lieder is thought to be the collection called *Winterreise.* Even though Schubert thought it was all too dark and depressing to be widely accepted.

When he was about twenty-one years old, Schubert left home. He moved in with friends. Schubert's friends were artists and poets. They introduced Schubert to new ideas.

B# **B SHARP:** Austria had a rule that all men had to serve in the army. But since Schubert was so short and had bad eyesight, he did not have to serve.

Schubert's Concerts

Schubert often played music for his friends. But no one else heard his songs. His friends decided to help him get recognition. They started hosting special parties. They called these parties "Schubertiads," or *Schubert events*. Schubert would play his music while his friends ate and danced.

B# **B SHARP:** The Schubertiads were very popular. But Schubert was never paid for any of these private concerts.

Beautiful Music

Schubert kept on composing during this time of private concerts. He wrote music for churches. He wrote **operettas**. He wrote music for plays. Schubert simply composed music all the time!

In 1825, Schubert wrote a piece called "Ave Maria." This beautiful song is often played in churches. "Ave Maria" is usually performed by one singer and a piano.

Beethoven's Biggest Fan

Schubert's favorite composer was Ludwig van Beethoven. Both composers lived in Vienna. People don't know if the two composers ever met. Schubert wrote that he once saw Beethoven in a restaurant but was too shy to talk to him.

Beethoven really liked Schubert's music. He said Schubert was a **genius**.

Beethoven died in 1827. Schubert carried one of the torches at his funeral, even though he himself was ill.

Schubert's Last Years

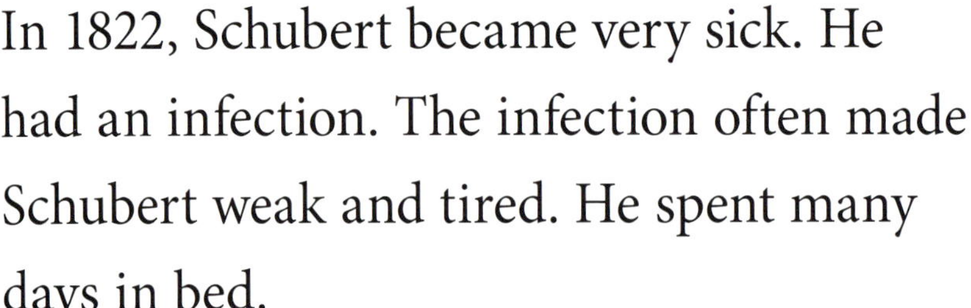

In 1822, Schubert became very sick. He had an infection. The infection often made Schubert weak and tired. He spent many days in bed.

But even when he was not feeling well, Schubert kept writing music. Schubert's health would be poor for the rest of his life.

In March 1828, Schubert held his first public concert. He played the piano. The concert also had a choir and a string quartet. Everyone who came loved Schubert's concert. But Schubert had bad luck.

A famous violinist named Niccolò Paganini played a concert that same night. All the newspapers wrote about Paganini's concert. They didn't mention Schubert at all.

Franz Schubert died on November 19, 1828. He was only 31 years old. Schubert wanted to be buried next to his idol Beethoven. And he was!

After Schubert died, his friends found many compositions in his home. One was called **Symphony** No. 8. Because Schubert did not finish the symphony, it is called "the Unfinished Symphony." It is now one of his most famous works. Like his other music, Schubert's Symphony is enjoyed and performed very often today.

Schubert's grave in Vienna.

Important Dates in Franz Shubert's Life

1797 Franz Peter Schubert is born on January 31 near Vienna.

1808 Schubert begins school at the Imperial and Royal Seminary.

1813 Schubert leaves school and becomes a teacher.

1818 Schubert stops teaching and leaves home.

1822 Schubert begins his Symphony No. 8; Schubert becomes ill and never finishes the new symphony.

1825 Schubert composes "Ave Maria" one of his best known compositions.

1827 Beethoven dies and Schubert carries a torch in the funeral procession.

1828 Schubert gives his last concert in March; he dies on November 19.

Glossary

cello a stringed instrument that makes a low sound

choir a group of people who sing together, often in a church or school

composer a person who writes music

conductor a person who leads an orchestra

genius someone who is very smart or creative

operettas short operas, often with funny themes

orchestra a group of instruments playing together

rival someone who competes with another person

string quartet a musical group made up of a cello, viola, and two violins

symphony a long piece of music written for a full orchestra

viola a stringed instrument with a lower sound than a violin

Read More About Schubert

Gerhard, Ann. *Curiosity Killed the Cat! Franz Schubert. (Little Stories of Great Composers)* The Secret Mountain, 2021.

McCully, Emily Arnold. *Our Little Mushroom.* Margaret K. McElderry Books, 2022.

Index

"Ave Maria" 22
conductor 13
Imperial and Royal Seminary. 11, 13
lieder 18
Mozart, Wolfgang Amadeus. 11
Paganini, Niccolò 29
Salieri, Antonio 11
Schubertiads. 20–21
Unfinished Symphony 30
van Beethoven, Ludwig 24–25, 30
Vienna. 6, 24, 30
violin 8, 13
Winterreisse 18